DTP PRINCIPLES

Better Documents By Design

I0408605

Improve your documents by understanding the design concepts, not just the software

DTP PRINCIPLES
Better Documents By Design

Improve your documents by understanding the design concepts, not just the software

by Richard Hallas

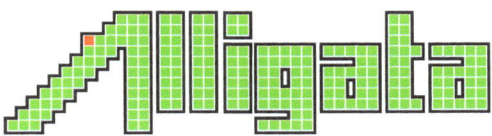

DTP Principles

Published by
David Bradforth
16 Rodney Way
Romford
Essex
RM7 8PD

Email: david.bradforth@alligatagroup.com

Printed by CreateSpace, an Amazon.com company.

Published by Alligata Media, Romford.

ISBN-13: 978-1503074989
ISBN-10: 1503074986

ABOUT THE AUTHOR

Richard Hallas was the editor of *RISC User* from volume 9 to volume 11. He was succeeded as editor by Mark Moxon for the final volume, for which he wrote within each issue then compiled the *RISC User: In a Nutshell* CD-ROM. Following this, he was responsible for the conception and launch of *Foundation RISC User* which he edited for its lifetime. DTP Principles consists of articles largely taken from the pages of *RISC User* and updated for this title.

DTP Principles has been previously published in magazine form.

INTRODUCTION

W elcome to *DTP Principles*, a special guide that tries to help DTP users improve the impact of documents by making informed design decisions.

Many special magazine features on DTP, as well as full handbooks on the subject, tend to concentrate on using the 'DTP package of the moment', or make a point of using one computer operating system at the expense of another. They generally concentrate on showing you how to produce fancy graphical layouts and eye-catching designs by using the latest and most advanced features that are available in the newest DTP software.

DTP Principles is different. You'll find nothing in this guide about individual DTP packages. You'll find nothing whatsoever about the choice of computer or operating system. You'll even find precious little about using the graphical features available in your choice of DTP package. What you will find, though, is plenty of information about how to make sensible decisions concerning the more fundamental aspects of your design, and how to treat your document's text with respect, so that your pages read impressively as well as looking good.

Flashy graphics and colourful layouts are all very well, but they're of little benefit if your text presentation lacks appropriate care and attention. This guide therefore discusses such matters as how to handle punctuation correctly, how to decide on line length and spacing, how to choose appropriate fonts for different situations, and lots of other text-related choices. The final section, on the Golden Ratio, presents some valuable information which is relevant to all aspects of design. There's lots to read, and I hope that even experienced DTP practitioners will find something of value here.

Richard Hallas

CONTENTS

1 · PLANNING A LAYOUT

When you sit down at your computer and load up a DTP package, the first step should be to have a good idea of what you want to achieve in mind before you start. It's very easy just to sit there and create a page, but unless you know fairly precisely the full range of uses to which your layout will be put, you may find yourself having to make extensive revisions—something which is tiresome in itself, and which detracts from your work if you want to have a consistent appearance, shared by several documents.

The fact is that, in most cases, page designs will be used for several pages in a document, and will often get reused for different documents, too; therefore they ought to be planned carefully from the outset. Even if you're designing only a single-page document such as a poster, you should

Figure 1: A two-column layout

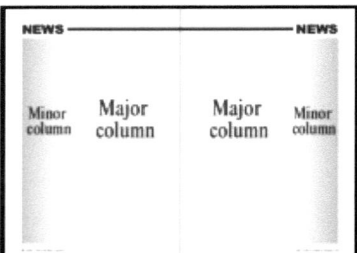

Figure 2: Two unequal columns

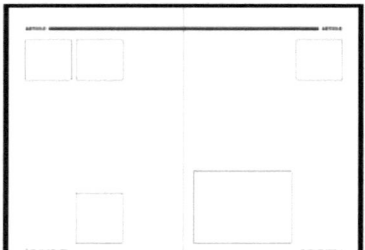

Figure 3: A three-column layout

spend time thinking about the effect you want to achieve before you start. Indeed, it's extremely important to plan the structure of posters carefully because, by their very nature, posters are supposed to be attention-grabbing.

So, when creating a page layout, it should be a case of 'art concealing art': the cleverness of the design should not be in the number of irregular frames you can fit onto the page to distract the reader's attention, but rather in how successful it is in concealing its own sophistication. By all means use the fancy effects available in your DTP package; just don't use them to excess!

SINGLE-COLUMN LAYOUTS

The simplest kind of layout is of course the single-column design. This is most commonly used for letters, smaller booklets, manuals, books and any text which the reader is expected to read continuously, without reference to illustrations. Generally, a single-column layout is most appropriate for text which is going to hold the attention for a long period, like a fictional story. In particular, single-column text needs careful tracking by the eye: the longer the line, the easier it is for the reader's eye to skip a line by accident, and so this is a good reason in itself (quite apart from other layout concerns) not to use single-column layouts for text which frequently requires the reader to refer to illustrations.

TWO COLUMNS

Two-column layouts are very useful for smaller (perhaps A5-size) magazines, and can provide a lot of flexibility. The most common form of such layouts is to have two columns of equal width. This is a good, flexible format: since the columns are not too wide, it's easy for the reader to refer to nearby illustrations when necessary, and the chances of skipping lines when reading are small. Also, positioning illustrations is easy as well, as they can take up the entire width of a column and may be placed quite freely on the page without breaking the text up in an ugly way (see figure 1).

But it's good to bear in mind that the two columns don't have to be of equal widths. For example, consider the news pages near the start of a magazine that you may be planning; figure 2 gives an

example of what they may look like. Here, the main stories (either the most important in terms of content, or just the most voluminous) are generally placed in the wider, 'major' columns in the centre of the facing pages. The outer, 'minor' columns, which are narrower and have background shading for contrast, are used to hold the shorter stories. That's not to say that important stories can't appear in the narrow columns as well, of course; but as a general rule the most significant items should appear in the wide columns under this particular design style.

So, the widths of columns can in themselves assign emphasis or importance to text. They can also be used in other ways. Two-column layouts can sometimes be used to house concurrent text. For example, think of a CD booklet containing an opera libretto: here, the original foreign-language text is likely to be in the first column, whilst the second column contains a translation. In such cases it's important for the text to be kept in step right the way through the document. It's also important that the two columns should not flow into one another; it would be a real nuisance if you had to type Italian in one column and then switch to English in mid-sentence as the caret moved into the second column! The two columns must instead be unlinked, so that typing beyond the end of any column causes a page break.

Finally, it's worth considering the case of the one-column/two-column hybrid. This is quite unusual, but can be very handy for certain documents. Here, the page design has two columns, but one is narrow and the other is wide (rather like the news pages example shown in figure 2). However, the two columns are unlinked (like a libretto): the inner, wide column is used for the main body text, whilst the outer, narrow column houses items which are peripheral to the main text, such as small illustrations, captions, comments or further explanations and clarifications. In other words, only the main, larger central column is used for the story, and the narrow column may provide nothing more than white space on some pages.

THREE COLUMNS

Like a two-column layout, a three-column design is very flexible, but in a different sort of way. You will not generally want to vary the relative widths of the three columns as you could with a two-column design. The flexibility comes in what you can do with illustrations. If you have some fairly small illustrations, then they can fit in the width of a single column; or if you have some large illustrations, they can be spread over two or even three columns. In all cases, though, they need not interfere with the main body text flowing around them (see figure 3). Some magazines or booklets may use both two- and three-column pages within the single publication, varying the number of columns to suit the purposes of the page contents. It's often the

This is a two-column text frame, and this text is in the first column. All the text in this frame has been set to snap to the baseline grid. Notice how the text aligns with all other text on this page.

A heading
See how the heading also aligns with all the other text on the page, and does not disturb the spacing of the following text.

This is the second column. The text within it aligns correctly not just with the text in the first column, but also with the text on the rest of the page.

Not only that, but because the heading in the first column, which is in a slightly larger font than the rest of the text, also snaps to the baseline grid, the text after it still aligns with the text in column two.

Figure 4 (above): The benefits of using a baseline grid and snapping body text and headings to it

This is a two-column text frame. The grid-snapping for all the text in this frame has been turned off. Notice how the text no longer aligns with the surrounding text in the main article.

A heading
See how the heading also fails to align with the rest of the text on the page, and also pushes the body text which follows it downwards, causing it to fail to align with the text in the second column as well.

This is the second column. Although the text within this two-column frame does not align with the other text in the main article, the two columns do at least align with each other.

But only up to a certain point! Look at what happens after the heading. Because the heading font is a little larger than the body text, and has a slightly taller line spacing, it has caused the text in these two columns to become misaligned.

Figure 5 (above right): The sorts of problems that you get when you fail to use a baseline grid

illustrations that finally determine whether a two- or three-column layout will be used, but sometimes it can be helpful to vary the number of columns to help make the text fit the amount of space available.

The drawback with three-column layouts is that the space available for the text can be a bit too narrow for comfort in smaller publications. If the page were only A5 in size, then three columns would very probably be too cramped and narrow to be useful. This does depend on the layout style, of course, and the size and nature of the body font in use; a condensed typeface would alleviate the problem to some extent. Even so, the use of relatively narrow columns does impact somewhat on the body text: it's usually the case that left-justified text looks excessively ragged when used within very narrow columns, and it can involve quite a lot of editing and rewriting work to overcome this. So, three-column layouts are really to be considered only for larger publications than A5, and A4 is probably the optimum size for such layouts.

Of course, you can play about with adding a 'spare' column for other things than the main text. For example, one idea that can work well is to have a page which is basically in two columns, but which has a third, outer column to house small illustrations and captions (like the one-column/two-column hybrid mentioned above).

FOUR OR MORE COLUMNS
Don't even consider using four columns unless you're working with at least an A4-sized page (and even A4 is probably too

small for four columns of body text). You'll need a fair amount of space to cope with so many columns, but, if you have it, they can be very flexible. Obviously they offer a great many options for sizing illustrations to multiples of a column, and indeed you can overlay tables or other box-outs on pairs of columns, or base entire two-column articles on a page which is divided into four columns overall. So, four-column layouts offer the maximum flexibility, but at a slight cost to the reader. Constantly moving the eyes from the top to the bottom of a page and back again does not make for relaxing reading, so if you do use a four-column layout, make sure you have plenty of illustrations to include, in order to provide some visual relief. A four-column page is one that lends itself to the inclusion of a number of shorter stories, rather than a single piece of text that flows right through it.

If you're considering more than four columns of body text then you're venturing into the realms of newspaper production, which is beyond the scope of this article!

BASELINE GRIDS
One much under-used but very valuable feature of professional DTP programs is the baseline grid. Rather than leaving the line spacing purely as a function of the text style, which is usually related to the size of the font, you can make your text (selectively, by style) snap to an invisible grid on the page. This has great advantages and few drawbacks: because you can define exactly which styles will use the grid, inappropriate text can be left to be sited freely, but all the most important text on the page (the body

text and related styles such as subheadings) can be made to align correctly with next to no effort. This is of the greatest importance, of course, with multi-column page layouts; if you're only using one column then a page grid is of little real benefit.

So, a baseline grid is an excellent means of getting a neat, consistent layout for your text, especially if the layout you are creating is strongly formalised, with a lot of body text, as it would be if you were planning a leaflet, booklet, manual, magazine or book. The booklet you're reading now is a good example of a strongly formalised document in which the baseline grid plays an important part. Documents which rely more on eye-catching design, such as posters, are generally not as suitable for a formalised grid, but they're in a relative minority. A grid can be a straitjacket if you let it be, but remember that not all your text styles have to use it, and if necessary you can turn the grid off locally even for styles which do snap to it by default. The only real disadvantage of a grid is that it adds more time to the initial planning of a layout; you have to be pretty sure of the text size and line spacing you're going to use from early on. But if you have a good idea about how you want your document to look right from the start, that shouldn't really be much of a problem: planning is definitely of the essence.

Figures 4 and 5 demonstrate some of the advantages that the grid provides, along with what can happen if you don't use it. Also consider the figures' captions: these do *not* snap to the baseline grid, because their text size is too small for the grid spacing.

Section 1 considered the different benefits of laying out text on pages containing two or more columns, and also the use of a baseline grid as a fundamental part of a page layout. The questions of how many columns to use, and whether to snap to a baseline grid, are very broad issues which are fundamental to the appearance of a document, and in this second section I want to focus on a matter which is more specific, but just as important when deciding upon the basic appearance of your work: the subject of words, lines and paragraphs, and the justification of text.

LINE LENGTH AND SIZE

When considering the number of columns you plan to use in your document, as discussed on the previous pages, one major consideration should be the size of the font you will be using for your body text. If you are using very small type then you should also use short lines in order to improve legibility. That may seem obvious, but it's an easy thing to overlook; the physical size of your page is only part of the equation, and by using very small type you are effectively increasing the size of the page in real terms. Think of what happens if you reduce an A3-sized page so that it can be previewed on an A4 sheet, for example: it may be physically A4-sized, but you will (or should!) have designed it with the A3 size in mind, so it won't actually 'work' at A4 size. By making your lines too long for the size of your type, you're effectively doing the same thing, so make sure that you bear the question of font size in mind when creating your initial multi-column layout. In general you should be aiming for something like ten words per line on average, which equates to around fifty to sixty characters.

The length of your lines and size of your body font also have a bearing on the line spacing. The default setting employed by most DTP packages of 120% line spacing (or a full line plus 20% of a line's worth of space) is reasonable, and for many purposes you can just accept that setting and forget about it. Nevertheless, if you care about making your text as clear and legible as possible, then you should consider whether it is really suitable for the work in hand. Shorter lines can stand having a smaller line spacing, and while you should never eliminate or negate the line spacing except to achieve special effects on occasion, you can take it

down to 110% quite comfortably for narrower columns. Equally well, if you need to use lines which are a bit excessively long, you should increase the line spacing in proportion, in order to make the text easier to read. Increasing the spacing minimises the chances of your readers' eyes skipping a line by accident. (Note that some DTP packages refer to 120% line spacing, whereas others may refer to 20% in exactly the same context because they assume that you won't ordinarily be making the spacing negative. In this instance, both figures mean exactly the same thing; just be aware of whether your chosen software considers 'no gap' to be 0% line spacing or 100% line spacing.)

So, in general you will want to pick a font and size which allows you to get the right number of words per page for your purposes, and the number of columns in your page layout will be governed to some extent by this choice. As I mentioned above, a reasonable average to aim for is around ten words, or up to sixty characters, per line. That can be considered an upper limit for most purposes, and you can use smaller values; for example, if you want a newspaper-style layout, you can use narrow columns and halve those values. The page you're reading right now is getting an average of eight words per line in its three-column layout, which equates to about forty-four characters per line.

Bear in mind, though, that you need to strike a reasonable balance between making lines too long for your reader to scan easily and making them so short that the reader's eyes have to do the equivalent of press-ups. If you find yourself in difficulties in terms of accommodating enough words on each line in a constricted space, consider changing your font: a more naturally condensed face will help, even if it's not a true condensed weight with 'condensed' in its name (and you could of course use one of those). Different fonts have different overall widths, and your choice of font is yet another factor which has a major impact on the characteristics of your page. However, choosing fonts is outside the scope of this article; section 7 discusses that topic in more detail.

All these considerations may seem awfully long-winded, and it's true that in many cases you can just accept the defaults presented to you by your DTP package. However, the experienced DTP practitioner will generally consider all of these factors as part of the design process, without

expending a great deal of conscious effort on them, and they are undoubtedly worth bearing in mind if you care about your work.

PARAGRAPHS

So, once you have considered all the factors governing your choice of font, type size, column width and line spacing, you're finally ready to start considering your paragraphs.

The idea of paragraphs is that they break up the text into convenient chunks which can be digested easily by your readers. They should generally express one main idea, or a small collection of related ideas, in a coherent way. Clearly, the number of paragraphs you use is in part a function of your writing style, but there are nevertheless some basic ideas relating to the use of paragraphs that you should bear in mind when creating a layout.

First of all, using too few paragraphs will deter your reader. If your paragraphs are too long on average, they will make the text appear impenetrable and unfriendly. In more technical articles this may not be a very important consideration; you just need to bear your readership in mind.

Using many paragraphs can make your page look more friendly and inviting. If you are using a significant amount of speech (involving direct quotations) within your text then you will find yourself using lots of paragraphs quite naturally, but you can use almost as many paragraphs in normal prose as for speech if you want to make your article appear chatty and approachable.

On the other hand, by doing this you run the risk of irritating your readers! A modern trend is to use lots of very short paragraphs to give a document impact, or 'punch'. However, this has led to the over-use of one-sentence paragraphs; in some publications (like the nastier tabloid newspapers) it's rare to find any paragraph which contains more than one sentence.

This is irritating.

It's condescending.

You're dumbing down.

Really.

Don't do it! It's all very well to try making your layout approachable and accessible to a non-specialised audience, but don't treat your readers like idiots if you can avoid it. A lot of American books in particular seem to fall into this trap. It may initially serve to make the book seem friendly and approachable, but I for one find that it wears my patience very thin very quickly.

JUSTIFYING YOURSELF

So, the question of how long to make your paragraphs in general is important, but that's quite a subtle consideration. More immediately apparent is the matter of how the text within the successive paragraphs should be laid out: will it be ranged to the left, or spaced out to fill the entire column; or will it be treated in a more novel way? I am of course referring to its *justification*.

• **Left justification** (or *ranged-left* text) This is the most common format. Consecutive lines of text align on the left, but their right-hand edges appear ragged because no extra space is inserted between words or letters to space them out.

• **Full justification** (or simply *justification*) This other very common format involves space being inserted between words (and sometimes letters) so that both the left- and right-hand edges of consecutive lines of text align in neat vertical columns. The booklet you're reading now uses fully-justified text, and relies mainly on word-spacing but also makes some limited use of letter-spacing in the body text as well.

• **Right justification** (or *ranged-right* text) This is rarely used for whole paragraphs. The left-hand edge of consecutive text lines is ragged, and they align instead at the right. Right-justified paragraphs may usefully be employed in placing a caption at the left of an illustration, for example, or to align contact details (address, telephone number etc.) in a letter. Of course, it is frequently useful to right-justify individual lines of text; for example, to insert a date into a letter, or to provide an attribution for a piece of text or quotation. However, extensive use of right-justified paragraphs is rare.

• **Centred text**
Again, this is fairly unusual for whole paragraphs, and its use means that both left- and right-hand ends of lines will be ragged. Centred text is most commonly used for major headings and some picture captions, or for simple posters or menus. Although the symmetrical appearance of centred paragraphs is pleasing, and the spacing between words is even, centred text should often be avoided as over-use tends to produce a simplistic or clichéd design.

So, for normal documents, your choice will be between left justification and full justification for your body text. Fully-justified text makes better use of space on the page, particularly if you are using two or more columns. However, it does introduce problems. For shorter lines you will find that large spaces start appearing between words and, if your columns are too narrow, this may lead to the notorious 'rivers of white' problem, in which the excessive spaces between words form rivulets which appear to flow down the page and make your text appear highly disjointed. In order to avoid these large spaces you are likely to find yourself relying on hyphenation to a much greater extent than you will if you use left-justified text. Also, use of fully-justified text may introduce the need for letter-spacing as well as word-spacing; letter-spacing is something you will only ever need in body text when using full justification.

Left-justified text is arguably preferable to full justification in many situations, as it does not demand the same amount of use of hyphenation, it looks freer and less as though an artificial order has been imposed on it, and it allows the text to retain its natural spacing, thereby making it as easy as possible to read. However, if you are using multiple columns, left-justified text can make those columns appear excessively ragged, and if you are flowing your text around illustrations, then the text-flow will only have an even appearance on the justified side of the text. The more columns you use, the greater the incentive you have for using fully-justified body text.

INTER-PARAGRAPH SPACING

The final big choice you face with regard to your paragraphs is how to space them out down the page and determine the way of distinguishing new paragraphs. ¶ You will normally have two choices: either you will leave a certain amount of space (perhaps a line) between consecutive paragraphs, or you will leave no gap but instead indent the first line of each new paragraph by a relatively small amount. ¶ There is in fact a third choice which I am using in this section: you can use the paragraph symbol to indicate where a new paragraph will start. This leads to multiple paragraphs forming a single, unbroken block of text. ¶ You see this approach in use very occasionally, particularly in trendy typographical magazines, but it's not very helpful to the reader, and I certainly wouldn't recommend it.

Leaving a line's space between paragraphs is perfectly acceptable, and can be useful if the text of an article is a bit short to fill the necessary space, for example. It also makes

for a nice, open, clean page which is easy for the reader to view. You can use a whole line to separate paragraphs or you may use less than a full line's space (say half a line); in the latter case, though, you won't be able to use a baseline grid, as only whole-line spacing will fit itself to the grid.

The other style, which is being used in this booklet, is to indent each new paragraph with a tab, and to have no extra space between consecutive paragraphs. This is more traditional than using line-spaces and is better for making text appear continuous, as well as helping to get a few more words on each page.

Traditionally, the size of the paragraph indentation should be the same as the width of an em (i.e. a capital M in whatever font you're using). However, modern DTP software doesn't really cater for this refinement, and it's normal these days just to use a value of a few millimetres, regardless of the current font. The precise width doesn't matter as long as the text looks balanced. This booklet uses an indentation of 4mm.

THIS SECTION LOOKS WRONG

There's one thing to watch out for when indenting paragraphs: you should not indent any paragraph that follows a subheading. It looks ugly and is technically incorrect.

Similarly, *don't* do what I have done here! The choice is between indentation and line-spacing: you should not do both together. The point is that the indentation is the means of identifying a new paragraph: if you space out your paragraphs instead of indenting them, there's no longer any need to indent them, so *don't* indent them! The line's space renders the indentation redundant: using both space and indentation together is an unnecessary belt-and-braces approach.

KEEP YOURSELF TIDY

Regardless of the justification you choose, there are a few problems to try to avoid, the most important of which are *widows* and *orphans*. A widow is a very short (often single-word) line at the end of a paragraph. An orphan is one of two things: either it's a widow which appears at the very top of a new column (i.e. it has flowed there from the previous column or page), or it's the first line of a new paragraph which occurs on the last line of a column or page. These terms are both imprecise and widely misunderstood, and different references may well give you conflicting definitions; so you can be forgiven for forgetting which is which! Whatever you call them, though, they can be hard to avoid, but you should attempt to tidy them up by rewriting as necessary.

3 ⁞ PUNCTUATION

One of the easiest ways of spotting an amateur DTP practitioner is to look at the use of punctuation and other 'special' characters in a document. The layout may seem excellent, and the graphics might be colourful and exciting, but all too often you will discover that the text – which, after all, is the most important element in the majority of printed material – has been left in a severely unpolished state. So, let's have a look at how to handle basic punctuation and some other special characters.

BASIC PUNCTUATION

Punctuation exists to divide up sentences into meaningful chunks, and to help make the text as clear and easy to read as possible. Unless you're trying to achieve a particular visual effect (which is a graphical issue), punctuation should be as unobtrusive as possible. The correct use of commas, full stops, semicolons and all the other punctuation marks (not forgetting dashes and brackets) is essential in order to get the right meaning across, and bad punctuation can make a passage very difficult to read. In extreme cases, it can actually alter the meaning completely. For example, consider the following string of words:

I don't like you I am annoyed

How would you punctuate this? Should it be:

I don't like you. I am annoyed.

which is confrontational; or should it be:

I don't; like you, I am annoyed.

which represents agreement?

So, good punctuation is essential to good writing, and should be just another subconscious element that helps your reader to digest your message more clearly. If you don't understand how to punctuate properly, there are numerous books on English grammar which explain the subject (and do note that there are regional differences; Americans punctuate somewhat differently from the British, for instance). This article merely considers some of the aspects of using punctuation marks.

APOSTROPHES

I'll start by getting on my soapbox. It often seems as though 95% of the English-speaking population is ignorant of how to use the apostrophe correctly. If you're one of those people, please look it up in a book about grammar! The rules are simple and

easy to learn, and yet the incorrect use of apostrophes is one of the most widespread problems that make work look amateurish. The best example of misuse of apostrophes is the word "its", yet the difference between "its" and "it's" is so easy to learn that it's amazing that anyone ever gets it wrong at all. Figure 1 tells you exactly when to use each.

---

it's = "it is" or "it has"
its = EVERY OTHER CASE!

There are NO exceptions!

Figure 1: Everything you ever wanted to know about "it's" and "its" but were afraid to ask

---

QUOTATION MARKS

The first and most obvious thing to say about quotation marks (or, more informally, speech marks) is that you should use the curly versions instead of the straight ones (feet and inch marks) that are more easily accessible on your keyboard.

The main choice you face is whether to use single or double quotation marks. Most people were taught to use double quotes for speech, but in fact the choice is yours. The double marks are quite wide, and can cause text to look ragged if used often, or in narrow columns, and in such cases using single quotes may be preferable. I personally like to use double quotes for direct quotation of speech, and single quotes for 'ideas' or 'implied speech' (or sometimes names), but it does depend to some extent on the job in hand. If you're quoting any apostrophes, double quotes avoid confusion. Whichever you use, though, there are two important things to remember:

"First of all, if you need to quote something 'within the quote' then you should use the other kind of quotation mark: single quotes within double ones, or *vice versa*.

"Secondly, if you are extending a single quotation over more than one paragraph, as I am doing here (this paragraph and the previous one), then there should be an opening quotation mark at the start of each successive paragraph. There should be only one closing quotation mark, though, right at the very end of the quotation."

As for where to place the marks if the quoted section ends with a punctuation mark, it depends on what's being quoted.

"Here I am quoting a complete clause," so the comma goes inside the quotes.

Here I am quoting 'a name or idea', so the name or idea itself is enclosed in the quotes, and not the comma.

This sentence includes a quotation of speech which finishes the actual sentence itself, "so the full stop needs to be enclosed within the quotes."

"Entire quoted sentences should have all other punctuation within the quotes themselves; the closing quote should be the last character, not the full stop that ends the sentence."

SINGLE QUOTES

You should beware of the fact that closing quotes use the same character as the apostrophe, as this can cause confusion. Apostrophes are widely used, whereas single quotes are relatively rare. DTP packages can sometimes (understandably) get mixed up between the two, with the result that you might get an opening single quote where you actually want a closing one. Be aware of this, and check your work carefully before printing to ensure that this hasn't happened.

The thing to bear in mind is that opening single quote characters are only ever used for the purpose of opening quotations, whereas the closing single mark has a dual purpose. Opening single quotes should *never* be used to indicate an abbreviation, as figure 2 demonstrates.

QUESTION MARKS

Question marks should only be used with direct questions. That may seem like stating the obvious, but it's not uncommon to see things like:

He asked why he should do it?

which, of course, is not a question; it's a statement (of the fact that a question was asked). Because it's a statement, it has to end with a full stop:

He asked why he should do it.

It wouldn't be a question unless written as:

He asked, "why should I do it?"

EXCLAMATION MARKS

Exclamation marks (not 'explanation' marks, as some people call them) should be used with caution, and not to excess. Only use one at the end of a sentence if you genuinely want to make it exclamatory, and try to avoid using them in too many successive

DTP WORLD *Convention '96* **DTP WORLD** *Convention '96*

Figure 2: The opening quote in the left version is an all-too-common mistake; it should be an apostrophe (closing quote), as in the version on the right

sentences. Although they can be used to indicate the presence of a joke (if the humour isn't entirely obvious), this is less than subtle. Also, try to avoid the use of exclamation marks in headings.

Never, under *any* circumstances, use two or more exclamation marks together! They're not a means of adding emphasis, so using several does not impart any extra humour to a sentence!!! The effect is usually just to convey to the reader a sense of rabid over-enthusiasm on the part of the writer.

PARENTHESES

Parentheses (or brackets) are a bit like quotation marks, in that they enclose things in pairs, but they're a little less confusing to use. The most common mistake with brackets is to put them on the wrong side of other punctuation.

If your brackets occur in the middle of a sentence (before a comma), the brackets should not enclose the comma because the comma relates to what's outside the brackets. Thus, "...sentence (before a comma,) the brackets..." would be wrong (quoting from above).

Similarly, if a sentence ends with a bracket then you should not enclose the final full stop, exclamation mark or whatever inside the brackets (as here). The key question is: does your sentence still read correctly if the bracketed section is removed? It should. Losing a bracketed section may mean that you impart less information, but it shouldn't affect what the sentence says.

The most common error with brackets is to enclose a complete sentence within the brackets but to leave the full stop floating outside them. (This is an example of incorrect bracketing).

(If a whole sentence is in brackets, then the full stop should also be in the brackets.)

COLONS

Some people think that colons end sentences. They don't: you should not normally follow a colon with a capital letter. If you end a paragraph with a colon, and then follow it with a number of bullet-points on consecutive lines (or other similar situations), then you'll probably want to capitalise these successive lines, which is fine. But if your colon occurs in mid-sentence, you should *not* capitalise the word that follows it.

In cases where you want to enumerate something after a colon, some people write

both a colon and a dash:– like that. Don't do it; there's no reason for it, and it's considered bad practice. (Typographers, being a racy bunch, refer to this pair of symbols as the 'typographic phallus'. I jest not.)

HYPHEN, DASH AND MINUS

Very few people take the trouble to use dashes correctly, largely because the hyphen is the only character that's conveniently accessible on the computer's keyboard.

However, hyphens should only really be used for (as the name suggests) hyphenation. When you want a dash to separate clauses, you should really use en- or em-dashes. There is no absolutely concrete rule about how to use these two kinds of dash. It's generally accepted that em-dashes—like these—should abut the two words that they join, and have no spaces on either side, whereas each en-dash should be enclosed – like this – by a pair of spaces.

How you use en- and em-dashes together, though, is largely a matter of personal taste. The convention I like to follow is to use en-dashes in pairs to separate out clauses – like this – in a similar way to brackets, whereas I use em-dashes singly to separate off part of a sentence—like this.

Finally, there's the minus sign. Although it looks much like an en-dash, it's a character in its own right. The minus sign is the same size and vertical position as the crossbar of the corresponding plus sign (-+-+-+-). In addition to their mathematical purpose, minus signs are often used for date ranges, as in 1685-1750, although en-dashes may be used for the same purpose: 1685–1750 (en-dashes don't balance as well, though).

The use of spaces with minus signs is important. If you want to write a negative number, there should be no space: –1. If you want to write a subtraction, there should be a space on either side: 3 – 2 = 1. There should be no spaces in date ranges.

ELLIPSES

An ellipsis is a series of three full stops, and there's a special character for it, so be sure to use it rather than typing three dots, as the spacing will look more even ('...' versus '...'—the former is the proper ellipsis).

Ellipses are normally used to indicate that something is missing from a sentence, often when quoting what a ... person has said. If used in this way, there should be a space on either side of the ellipsis. However,

sometimes (particularly in less formal writing) it's desirable to use an ellipsis to indicate a trailing sentence... In this case, the ellipsis replaces the full stop, and should not be preceded by a space. (Occasionally an ellipsis can start a sentence, and it shouldn't have a space associated with it then, either.)

SPACES

Do spaces qualify as punctuation? Regardless of whether or not they do, they certainly have an effect on the other punctuation in your text.

There are two ways in which spaces are often used incorrectly. One is to separate punctuation from the words to which it relates; the second is to insert excessive space between sentences or clauses.

Does this paragraph look OK to you ? It certainly doesn't look right to me . In it I have inserted one space between punctuation marks , and two spaces at the end of every sentence and clause; this is something you see quite often .

Punctuation marks are generally intended to abut against the word(s) to which they relate; so you should not insert a space before a question mark, or a full stop, or any other common punctuation mark. A small number of general-purpose marks *can* have a space on either side, but these are the 'double sided' ones, such as dashes and ellipses, which are intended to span between words, and the way spaces are used with them is significant (as explained above).

More controversially, you should *not* use two spaces between sentences and clauses. Lots of people have been taught to use two spaces at the ends of sentences, but it's a hangover from the days of the typewriter (as is underlining), and is bad typographic practice. You may find very occasionally that it's necessary to use a double space in order to avoid a clash of letters in a particular font (and this is most likely with a condensed face), but that's a practical matter. For normal use, double spaces should be avoided.

Figure 3: The five most common ligatures

LIGATURES

A nice finishing touch is to use ligatures (fi and fl) in place of the separate letters. Use the ff, ffi and ffl ligatures, too, if your font has an expert set (the body font in use in this booklet does not). Serif fonts are more likely to have expert sets; figure 3 shows what the five most common ligatures look like.

So far I've been talking about the choices you face when planning a layout: how many columns to use, whether to snap to a baseline grid, and how to space out lines and justify paragraphs. These topics are all fundamental to a balanced and well-presented document, and in this section I want to look at a couple of other elements that relate closely to the text itself: headings and drop-caps.

HEADINGS

The subject of headings may sound trivial, but there are actually many things to consider when deciding what forms your headings will take, and they can have a major impact on the appearance of your document.

FONTS FOR HEADINGS

First of all, the choice of font is extremely important. The subject of fonts is of course fundamental to DTP, and a topic for another section. For the moment we can ignore the finer details: the real choice is whether to use a serif typeface, a sans-serif face or a display font. This choice is largely governed by the number and size of headings that you expect to use in your document.

If all you need is a big, eye-catching title for an article, and perhaps one smaller subheading style to be interspersed within the text, then you might like to experiment with a display font for your main title or headline. Display fonts – that is, the sorts of fancy designs that look interesting and fun but which you wouldn't dream of using to set body text – are ideal for use with large headings, titles and other pieces of 'one-off' text; that's what they're for. Such fonts can add lots of visual interest to a document, but you should try to ensure that they don't look too out of place. A layout which is serious and formal can easily become silly and gimmicky if you use an inappropriate display font within it. Ideally, your choice of display font should reflect the tone and style of your document and, if possible, be balanced by other graphical elements elsewhere on the same page. Display fonts can of course be used with formal documents; a font doesn't have to be 'silly' to be 'fancy'! If you do use one, though, it should be appropriate to your design, and you stand more chance of making a page look silly by an inappropriate choice of display font than by simply playing safe and using a sans-serif or serif face.

That's not an excuse to play safe, though! Experimentation counts for a lot when choosing fonts for any document. A display font has been used for the headings in this booklet (EFF Mackintosh: a tribute to the style of Charles Rennie Mackintosh), and its quirky use of dots and dashes has been reflected in other elements on the page.

You may choose not to use a display font, either because it seems inappropriate to do so or because you need several different heading styles. If you do need to use a range of different styles of heading in a single document (such as two or more sizes for article titles, plus major and minor subheadings within articles) then it's better to take a more consistent approach: use just one well-specified font family for all of your headings, but give them plenty of variety. For instance, the most important headings could be all in capitals, whilst the least important subheadings could use a condensed weight. Remember too that many fonts include weights which were designed to be used as headings, even though you wouldn't class them as display faces as such. (Surely no-one reading this article thought that Gill Sans Ultra-Bold was intended for use as body text,

---

Have you ever thought about the space that comes after a drop-cap? If the dropped letter is the first letter in a word, then surely the other letters in the word should run up to it, whereas the words on the subsequent lines need a bigger separation. DTP packages do not usually cater for this situation, but you can fool them by use of hard spaces or soft carriage returns on subsequent lines.

FEEL FREE to be daring and extrovert with your drop-cap! It doesn't have to be in the same font or style as the rest of the paragraph; use the same fancy display font as in your article title if you wish, and, if some colour is available, consider picking it out in a spot colour. Such fancy drop-caps work better over five lines or more.

A DROP-CAP which is a word in its own right should really have an extra space after it; the converse of the case above. However, that's a mixed blessing: if the drop-cap is a letter I then it's OK, but if it's an A, as here, then the space which is a part of the letter itself works against the real space that comes after it, and makes the total amount of space look far too great.

There are occasions when you need to italicise the first word in the paragraph with the drop-cap, and so you may choose to make the drop-cap italic as well. Just be careful when doing this, as it may be necessary to insert extra spaces to prevent collisions with the cap. In this paragraph, it was necessary to insert an extra space between the 'dropped T' and the following 'here'.

Figure 1: Four examples of using dropped capitals (also known as drop-caps or initial capitals)

for example!) Some fonts even go so far as having 'Title' or 'Titling' in their names.

Generally speaking, it's a good idea to set headings in a sans-serif face, even if your body text is a serif font. The serifs are there to make long stretches of text easier to read, but that doesn't matter for headings, and if you're using a serif body font, a sans-serif headings font will add contrast. Sans-serif fonts are generally better at looking bold and standing out than serif ones, and they also look more modern and crisp; these are both good reasons to use them for headings. There's nothing wrong with using serif faces as headings, of course, but they will lend an old-fashioned or traditional air to your document (which may be what you want).

If your document includes captioned illustrations, then you'll probably also want to use a headings font variant for the captions.

THE IMPACT OF HEADINGS

The important point to keep in mind at all times, though, is that the purpose of headings is to have visual impact. In other words they need to be either bold, attention-grabbing, or both. If you use a fancy display font, then the attention-grabbing aspect is taken care of automatically; but if you don't (and in most cases you probably won't), then make sure that your headings font provides plenty of contrast with the text surrounding it. Using an italic version of the body text is surprisingly common, but it's no good: such headings will just get lost on the page, and will not serve their purpose of providing a visual anchor. On the other hand you shouldn't go totally overboard: if you're using a very light body font, don't use ultra-bold headings! Keep balance in mind at all times and make your headings obvious without letting them become a distraction. That will often, but not always, mean that you're using at least the Bold weight.

Once you've got a font that provides contrast, the size you should use comes into question. The smallest subheadings should either be the same point size as your body text or just a little larger. Work from the bottom up: start with your body text size, or something a couple of points bigger, for your least important style of heading, and then for each successive heading style that you need, make it 50% to 60% larger than the last. That's a very rough guide; you'll need to modify the sizes to look right with the font you've chosen, and you'll need to miss out some intermediate sizes if you only use a couple of sizes of heading. Nevertheless, it's a reasonable general rule to follow.

Finally, consider the text styles that you apply to your various headings. For the most important headings, as well as being large

and bold, it's often a good idea to put the text entirely in capitals; though an all-caps heading should be kept relatively short. Use of small capitals instead of lower-case letters can also be effective for headings of medium importance. Some authorities recommend the use of letter spacing in headings, but I don't think this is effective very often, so I wouldn't normally advise it. In fact, I consider that letter spacing should be avoided under normal circumstances even in body text; I have used it in this booklet because of the nature of the layout, which uses a condensed body font, but normally I would avoid it. Font designers are very careful to create balanced spacings between letters, and one should be wary of contravening their design decisions.

For subheadings within the body text, condensed fonts can be very useful. For headings which are not in all-caps, consider your capitalisation rules: are you going to capitalise every word, all the important words, or just the first word of the heading? You should avoid over-use of capitals in all but the most important headings, though.

If your headings run to more than one line, try to balance the line-lengths as much as you can, starting with the longest lines at the top and getting progressively narrower.

DROP-CAPS

The purpose of 'dropped capitals' (or *drop-caps* for short; they're also sometimes referred to as *initial capitals*) is not only decorative. It's true that one of their purposes is to provide visual interest (and as such the best examples are the illuminated capitals found in manuscripts of the Middle Ages), but in fact their main function is to show the reader where the main text starts. As such, they should not be over-used: in general, if you use drop-caps at all, you should have a single drop-cap at the very start of an article, or one to start each chapter of a book. Don't use them to start each subsection within a single article; even for major subsections. They should be reserved just for the very beginning.

Another important point is that you shouldn't use a drop-cap directly after a heading. That goes without saying if you're only using a drop-cap at the start of an article, but you may occasionally need to begin an article with a subheading. If this is the case, then don't use a drop-cap as well.

Figure 2: *An die Musik* by Franz Schober; note that drop-caps don't always have to be 'dropped' (upper example); they may even have their associated text overlaid if the font is suitably florid (lower example)

As with most rules, there's the odd exception: drop-caps can occasionally be useful for special effects, such as printing questions and answers with large Q and A indentations, or illustrating step-by-step instructions with dropped numerals. For these purposes, drop-caps are acceptable within body text and following headings.

Drop-caps should generally be at least three lines high, and the choice is normally from three to five lines. Sometimes you see them extend to seven or more lines, but very large drop-caps can be cumbersome; their use depends on the document and font, and whether you're making a design statement.

The four examples in figure 1 illustrate some of the practical concerns surrounding the use of drop-caps. It may be argued that, depending on whether the drop-cap is itself a whole word, extra spaces should be inserted to make the fact clear, as shown in the two left-hand examples. This question is valid, but tends to be ignored these days; most people just leave the text as it is, and don't worry about such refinements. Besides, inserting spaces is unreliable (particularly if you later do something which causes words adjacent to the drop-cap to change position).

When using drop-caps, it's quite common to capitalise the un-dropped letters of the first word of the paragraph, or the first few words, or even the entire first line. This is done supposedly in order to make the alignment of the top of the drop-cap neater against the tops of the first row of letters, but it's entirely optional. As drop-caps can be used to create artistic effects, at times you'll want to place them manually, as in figure 2.

Hyphenation is one of those things that can cause a lot of problems if you let it. It's something that DTP packages often have trouble getting just right, so if you use hyphenation in your documents at all, you should keep a conscious eye on what's happening to make sure you're happy with what your software is doing.

Received wisdom informs us that hyphenation has no effect on the clarity of text, and does not impair the speed and fluency with which we read. I have to say that I'm not at all convinced by that assertion; I have personally never liked hyphenation very much, and almost never use it in my documents by default, although I may hyphenate a single, particularly long word on occasion if a paragraph would look too ragged without it. I do find, though, that split words at the ends of lines disrupt the flow of the text for me, so I always make sure that hyphenation is off; apart from anything else, it avoids the possibility of slips such as unnoticed but inappropriate hyphenation creeping in.

If you don't agree with me, though (and it's largely a matter of personal taste), you may want to turn automatic hyphenation on. There's no doubt that it makes your life somewhat easier; if your DTP package can insert hyphens wherever it deems them appropriate, you will largely avoid the problem of excessively ragged paragraph edges (or large amounts of white space between words in fully justified text). Consequently you will have to do much less rewriting work than if you were striving manually to make your paragraphs look presentable, which is what I generally do. The only penalty is all those little hyphenation marks at the ends of lines (and, of course, you'll have to remember to read your text through again to check the hyphenation).

So, if you're going to use hyphenation, what do you have to watch out for, and what control can you exert over what goes on? Here's a summary.

THE BASIC PROBLEMS

In order to hyphenate words successfully, DTP packages need some way of knowing where any given word can be split. The way they decide how to do it depends partly on algorithms and partly on being told explicitly how specific words can be broken up, because no algorithm can hope to work absolutely faultlessly.

Even when using software in which the hyphenation rules are sophisticated and work well, you must watch out for certain problems. The most potentially embarrassing is the rude word syndrome: a surprisingly large number of perfectly innocuous words can be split in such a way that the result has undesirable implications (even though you may grab more of your readers' attention than would otherwise be the case!). Figure 1 demonstrates this in newspaper headline style. The headlines are contrived, but they're plausible errors even so, and the examples are valid (in that real software will hyphenate these words in this way under the right conditions). It would of course look grossly unprofessional to print a heading in which the last word was split over two lines, as in the second example, so this headline would be unlikely to crop up in real life; but if you ever use 'arsenal' in mid-sentence, watch out!

The other main problem is that of over-hyphenation, where too many lines in a paragraph are hyphenated, often needlessly. The good news is that this problem can largely be avoided by setting up sensible defaults in your software but, even so, you should keep a watchful eye on what the software is doing.

WHAT CAN BE DONE?

The first thing that you can to do avoid such problems is to set up sensible hyphenation options. Your software may not, by default, hyphenate words of five letters or fewer, and it's unlikely to split words one letter from their beginning or end. You may be able to tell it not to hyphenate more than a certain number of consecutive lines in a paragraph. Used together, such settings avoid many problems.

Not all software will give you such fine control over the way it works, though. Nevertheless, almost all DTP and word

processing software allows you to edit the hyphenation exception dictionary to tell the program which words should not be split, or to tell it appropriate places in which to break specific words. Of the predefined exceptions in such dictionaries, you will be bound to find many that have been included to avoid the rude word syndrome. You might like to define some other ones if they're not there already (for instance, 'arsenal', 'bravery' and 'therapist') so these words may not be split.

By including hyphens in the exception definitions, you should be able to tell your software exactly where it may split a word. Some programs allow you to give such hyphens priorities, but other software may not support this refinement, and all you can do then is to tell the application the appropriate places where splits may occur. All software should allow you to define words which will never be hyphenated, though.

MANUAL HYPHENATION

Regardless of whether you are using automatic hyphenation, when you type hyphens into text directly, the software will use your hyphens to split the words at the ends of lines. You may not always want this to happen. For example, if you use 'e-mail' (I happen to prefer 'email') then you won't want it to be split at the hyphen when it falls at the end of a line. The solution is to use a hard hyphen: like a hard space, this will always be printed, and the software should never allow a line-break to occur at the hyphen's position.

Conversely, you may want to tell your DTP software where to split a specific instance of a word, but not to hyphenate it explicitly. In that case you would use a soft hyphen. If a word containing a soft hyphen appears at the end of a line, then it will split at the place you have specified (and print the hyphen); if, however, reformatting causes the word to change position such that it no longer needs to split, the soft hyphen will become invisible. It's extremely common to come across documents that contain words with visible hyphens within them, like this: hyphen-ation. This error occurs when the designer has used a standard hyphen and the text has then reflowed such that the hyphenated word no longer appears at the end of a line. Pay careful attention to such things: this problem is very common (and distracting for the reader), and can be avoided entirely by the proper use of soft hyphens.

HUSBAND IN BRA-VERY TOP AWARD

Figure 1: How not to hyphenate your headlines! By editing the hyphenation exception dictionary, the rude word syndrome can be avoided

NEW FLU VACCINE IN DOCTOR'S ARSE-NAL

One of the most important things that really defines how your document looks, and lays the foundation for your text's message, is your choice of font. Unfortunately, choosing fonts that are effective and appropriate to the subject material is no simple matter.

The subject of fonts is a huge one; more than enough to fill a book, let alone a short article. This introduction begins by explaining how to recognise the categories into which fonts fall, as an understanding of fonts is essential for good typography and DTP, even if it all seems a little esoteric. It then goes on to look beyond the family categories, at design elements within particular type styles.

CLASSES OF TYPEFACE

Font families obviously come in a vast range of styles, but these styles can be broken down into just a few categories, as follows:

Bembo
Garamond
Plantin
Old style • AEIOU aeiou

Old style

In the earliest days of printing (in the latter half of the 15th century), no-one thought of fonts as a means of artistic expression, and they didn't do gimmicky things like designing letters with snow on top for Christmas cards. The earliest fonts were designed to make books (of which there were few, and they were generally Bibles, prayer books and so on) as legible as possible.

As a result, those fonts are still in widespread use today because of their clarity and elegance. No-one cares that they're half a millennium old; they're still wonderfully legible, and make trendy new fonts look as ephemeral as they really are. They contain no design gimmicks to jab you in the eye.

Old style fonts have a pleasing mixture of thick and thin strokes (with moderate but not excessive contrast between widths) which developed out of the way scribes drew letters. They always have serifs, which are bracketed (joined to the main strokes with a curve) and, in lower-case characters, angled.

Rounded letters have a diagonal stress, which means that the weighting between thick and thin portions of the strokes is at an angle (top-left to bottom-right).

Baskerville
Times New Roman
Utopia
Transitional • AEIOU aeiou

Transitional

Transitional fonts emerged in the late 17th century in an attempt to improve on existing, classic faces, and they form an intermediate stage between old and modern type styles. Transitional fonts have a stronger contrast between strokes than their predecessors, and the stress in curved letters may be vertical (or less obviously slanted). Serifs also tend to be sharper, but retain their brackets and their angles on lower-case letters. Old style and transitional faces can sometimes be difficult to tell apart.

Bodoni
Ellington
Century
Modern • AEIOU aeiou

Modern

So-called *modern* fonts began to appear at the turn of the 17th and 18th centuries, taking the elements of transitional designs to their extremes. In modern faces, the emphasis is on formal structure, and elegance and legibility are less of a concern. That's not to say that they are inelegant, but the elegance is of a different nature. The ties with handwriting are minimal, and the emphasis is on structural clarity. The result is a style which looks very clean, but which is also rather formal. Modern faces are characterised by a very high (sometimes extreme) contrast between thick and thin strokes, a vertical stress in curved letters,

and very thin, absolutely horizontal serifs with no brackets (or at most very small ones).

Clarendon
Joanna
Rockwell
Slab serif • AEIOU aeiou

Slab serif

Slab serif fonts (also sometimes referred to as *Egyptian* faces) began to appear in the early 19th century as a result of the rise in advertising. Clean, bold fonts were needed to catch the eye rather than to be read in large quantities. At first, designers tried to produce heavier versions of modern fonts with fattened serifs, but this didn't always produce good results, and so the stroke contrast was eliminated entirely in some slab serif fonts.

So, slab serif fonts, as their name implies, feature heavy, slab-like serifs. The serifs will be horizontal and will have little bracketing (if any). Strokes may have some thick and thin contrast or may be of equal width. Any stress in rounded letters is vertical.

Futura
Gill Sans
Optima
Sans-serif • AEIOU aeiou

Sans-serif

The first *sans-serif* ("without serif") typeface was designed by William Caslon IV in 1816. However, it was not an instant success, and although the sans-serif style began to pick up in popularity through the 19th century, it was not until the 1920s that the style came into its own, thanks to the Bauhaus school of design. Claimed to be "type of the future", and following the Bauhaus idea that "form follows function", sans-serif (also known as *Grotesque* or *Gothic*) faces stripped type

Gaßenbelchiges Qualitätsbier
Black letter (Fette Fraktur)

Dear John... CURIOSITY...
Script (Freestyle)   Display (Malinka the Cat)

down to its bare essentials: all unnecessary appendages were removed from the letters.

Therefore it goes without saying that sans-serif fonts have no serifs at all, and will have little or no contrast in stroke thickness. They also have a tendency towards a greater x-height than serif faces. Sans-serif faces are sometimes broken into two sub-styes: *Geometric* and *Humanist*. Geometric faces are constructed from regular shapes, and the bowls of their curved letters will be close to circular. Humanist faces will have a slight contrast between thick and thin strokes, or possibly slightly fluted strokes. The stress in sans-serif fonts, if present at all, is vertical.

OTHER KINDS OF FACES
In addition, there are other kinds of font which do not fit into the above categories.

Script
So-called *script* fonts are those that directly mimic handwriting, and as a group are not tied to any specific period of history (although some specific types of script are, of course). They cover a variety of styles, such as black letter faces, calligraphic writing and drafting scripts (used by architects and some cartoonists). The only thing they have in common is that they appear to have been written by hand.

Black letter
Black letter fonts are the oldest types, and are often put in a class of their own, but really they are a kind of script, as they mimic the hands used by scribes before printing was invented. Black letter faces have traditionally been particularly popular in Germany. (The Germans, also being rather fond of beer, tended to mix the two, giving rise to some rather attractive labels.)

Display
Often referred to as *fancy* fonts, *display* faces are the fun fonts that we all like to use when the opportunity presents itself. Display faces are intended to be eye-catching, for use in advertisements or large headings, and range from very heavy fonts that you would use just for titles to the kinds that include gimmicky elements that make them suitable only for very specific purposes. Some of the most common 'gimmick' display faces are the aforementioned snow-capped ones that always make their presence felt on home-grown Christmas cards; but there are many others in the same category (such as ones made up of acrobats, cats, animals, fruit, medical equipment, letters in fancy dress and so on). The more generally useful display faces are the ones that are purely decorative.

One particular family of display font that's worth mentioning is *grunge* type (also known variously as *fringe*, *deconstructive*, *edge*, *anarchic* type or several other minority monikers; I just call them hideous). These fonts started to appear soon after the DTP revolution got underway, when ordinary users found themselves able to create fonts of their own. Grunge fonts are currently highly popular with typographers, despite the fact that the DTP revolution has been a part of everyday life for several years now. The only characteristic that links grunge fonts is that they are guaranteed to be almost impossible to read. People generally either love them or hate them; typographers seem to take them a lot more seriously than one might expect.

Monospaced
As their name suggests, *monospaced* fonts are those whose characters are all of equal width. They're useful for numbers in tables and other situations where variable-width

characters are not wanted (such as computer program listings). As computers are a lot cleverer than typewriters, though, you don't often need monospaced fonts in normal DTP.

Symbol
Finally, *symbol* fonts cover anything that isn't comprised of letters and numbers. The most famous symbol font is Dingbats, but there are lots, for music, cartography, semaphore, Morse Code and many other things.

FONT ANATOMY
All this background information may seem slightly irrelevant, but being able to identify the features and classes of fonts is the first step toward their enlightened use. Having an understanding of the structure of a font's characters is also an important asset when deciding on which typeface to use for a project, so the rest of this article will examine the component parts of fonts and put names to the elements that make them distinctive.

VARIATIONS ON A THEME
Many people think that the number of fonts available is ridiculous. After all, they say, who needs hundreds of fonts with confusing names, most of which look almost identical?

These people are missing the point to some extent. Whilst it may be fair comment to say that most users don't need such a vast quantity of fonts as professional designers, and that many fonts do look superficially similar, the fact is that, if you look closely, you will find that very few fonts are hard to tell apart. Most have a very clear character of their own; all you have to do is use your eyes!

Of course, some people get carried away; there's no surer way to bore your friends than to be able to identify any font at ten paces. But you don't have to be a born-again train-spotter to appreciate the artistic beauty of a well-crafted typeface; all you need is a basic interest and a few labels to help identify the constituent parts of a letter so you can judge how the different aspects of character design vary between fonts.

BODY PARTS
Have a look at figure 1. It shows a typical old style font (Monotype Sabon). Notice its old style nature: the moderate contrast between strokes, angled, bracketed serifs, and the diagonal stress in rounded letters.

There are several lines running across figure 1, relating to the vertical position of the various font elements. When using different fonts in your documents, the only line that will stay the same is the baseline, on which the letters sit. The others are totally arbitrary, and indeed the ascender line and capital line will often be the same.

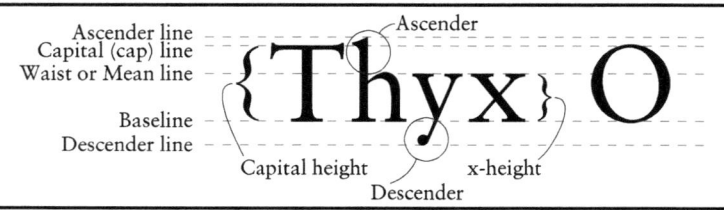

Figure 1: The various horizontal lines within a font, along which serifs will guide your eyes. In many fonts the ascender line and cap line are the same, but some fonts have ascenders which are taller than their capital letters. In classic fonts, the waist line will often be at the Golden Section between the baseline and cap line

In fact, in a small number of cases, there may not even be a descender line, if the type designer has made the decision not to have any descenders in his letters. But what you see in the figure is the norm: a well-balanced font with its design elements clearly distinguishable. There are a few points worth noting: the lines apply to the main parts of the letters, not to their serifs (so the vertical serifs on the crossbar of the 'T' protrude above the cap line). Curved letters also extend slightly beyond the cap, waist and baseline to achieve optical balance (look at letters 'O' and 'h'). Also, the waist line will be about two-thirds of the way up between the baseline and cap line. In fact, in many cases it will fall on, or close to, the Golden Section (61·8% between the two lines; see section 8). This is by no means universal, but it's very common, and helps a design look balanced.

The most important measurement in figure 1 is the x-height (which determines the position of the waist line). In normal usage (i.e. unless you're working entirely in capitals, which is unlikely), it is the x-height of a font that determines its visual size. People normally refer to font sizes by saying things like 14pt, 18pt or whatever, but unfortunately this is not as helpful as it might be. In the days of 'real' typesetting, when the type was made of little metal blocks, the point size referred to the size of the block on which the character was created, which would be somewhat greater than the physical bounding box of any given character in the font. Within that size, the type designer could create whatever he liked, and could choose not to use all the available space. So, some fonts are significantly larger than others at any given size. Try comparing a few fonts side by side to see for yourself. Moreover, the larger the x-height of a font, the bigger it seems to be at any point size, as it's the height of lower case letters that usually accounts for how large a font looks. So, when choosing a font, you need to bear these things in mind, as they will have a major impact on the look of your page.

Figure 2 shows what the various bits of letters are called. As in figure 1, the font is Monotype Sabon, because an elegant old style face demonstrates design elements that are less likely to be present in more modern styles. Besides, most body fonts in use today are actually old style faces.

When referring to parts of characters, there's a point of contention that's worth noting. People sometimes call letters' tails 'swashes' (Q being the obvious example). That isn't right: a swash is a florid addition to a letter, used for artistic effect. If the tail is part of the normal letter design, then it's

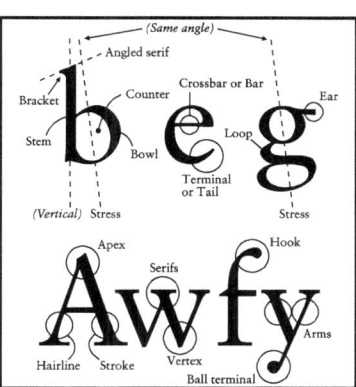

called a tail. Swashes are ornaments, used sparingly to add extra decoration to individual characters (such as initial capitals).

Figure 3 demonstrates what happens when you put a roman font into italics. As you can see, the change with a serif font is much more striking than with a sans-serif face. The lower-case 'a' loses its two-storey design in favour of a single-storey form, the upper arm of the 'k' turns into a loop, and the characters in general become more like the scripts from which they were originally derived. Sans-serif faces owe relatively little to 'real' handwriting, as those ties had largely been broken by the time that sans-serif faces started to appear. So, in many cases, the 'sloping' version of a sans-serif face is actually an oblique version of the roman font, which means that, apart from being slanted, it's identical. The term 'italic' implies that the letter designs are different from the roman. In the 20th Century font shown in figure 3, the slanted font is in fact a true italic, in that the letter shapes have been subtly adapted. Even so, the changes

are hard to spot. Few sans-serif typefaces have strikingly different italics.

To round off, look at figure 4 and see what happens as a font increases in boldness. The 20th Century font has many weights, and although the strokes get gradually thicker as the boldness increases, the overall height stays constant. The general progression is not uniform, as you can see from the relative word lengths shown in figure 4. Each weight has been crafted carefully so that it is well balanced in itself: the lightest weight needs sufficient space between letters to allow them to be seen clearly without their strokes causing a dazzle, and so it actually prints out wider than the next heaviest weight.

This section has been about revealing detail that is often missed, and learning to appreciate it, but it's not necessary for most people to know more about fonts. If you are interested in fonts and typography, though, I would particularly recommend *The Elements of Typographic Style* by Robert Bringhurst (Hartley & Marks, ISBN 0-88179-132-6).

Figure 3: A comparison of Roman and Italic faces in serif and sans-serif fonts. The font on the left is Sabon; the other is 20th Century. Both are true italic faces (rather than oblique), but the differences are much less pronounced in the sans-serif design

Figure 4: Seven weights of Monotype 20th Century. Notice how the increasing boldness is achieved by the careful thickening of strokes, and how this increasing thickness is more pronounced horizontally rather than vertically

In the previous section I described some important aspects of typefaces: the broad classifications into which they fall, and the component parts that make up the letters. Even if it all seemed a bit esoteric at first sight, it's important because it's necessary to understand something about these things in order to make an informed choice about the fonts you intend to use in any project. You can't just take a 'pin the tail on the donkey' approach when choosing fonts; if you are serious about the end product, and care how your work looks, then you need to spend time thinking about which fonts will help you convey the message you want to put across, or which work best with your design.

Having said all that, though, choosing fonts is by no means an easy task, and it's also a very personal decision. I can't lay down the law on what's right and wrong; all I can do here is to point out some of the things that you should consider when planning your design. Thousands of fonts are available for the DTP practitioner to use these days. That's good because it means that there's a huge range of choice in any given style; and it's also bad for the same reason. How do you pick which font is best out of maybe hundreds of similar designs? It's all a matter of experience, and the answer will be unique to any given individual in any case. You can, however, narrow the choice down.

FONT CLASSIFICATION

What category does your current project fall into? Is it an eye-catching poster that needs to use decorative fonts to get its message across? Is it a book, or booklet, which contains a lot of text that needs to be as easily readable as possible? Is it a brochure which contains a limited amount of text that must be both eye-catching and legible? All of these basic, broad questions should have a lot of impact on the font you decide to use, and allow you to narrow down your choices into font categories from the very start. The various kinds of font all lend themselves to different purposes.

Old style: the very earliest fonts were designed exclusively for use in books, and hence are ideal for setting long passages of text which is meant to be read easily and fluently. Their elegance makes such ancient fonts as useful today as when they were first designed, hundreds of years ago. (Of course, not all 'old style' faces are ancient, but that's beside the point; it's the design

style that matters.) The fact that their designs are devoid of eccentric quirks makes them 'invisible' to the reader: design characteristics which make many fonts clearly identifiable and individual also serve to make the reader more aware of them. Old style faces are generally free of such individualistic traits, and are hence more legible in long passages than any other kind of font.

So, if your project contains a large amount of text which the reader is expected to read and digest, such as a book or substantial newsletter, you should definitely use a serif font, and using an old style face is likely to be a good idea. Conversely, large bodies of closely packed and impersonal text can look imposing or characterless, so if your project is less austere, an old style face may not be the best choice.

Transitional: for the purposes of this article, transitional fonts can be grouped with modern fonts. They are generally slightly less well suited to lengthy passages of text than old style faces, but it does depend on the font; some are perfectly suitable, and it's unlikely that you'd ever be fired for setting a book in Times New Roman (even though it wouldn't be a particularly imaginative choice).

Modern: in contrast with the highly legible old style serif fonts, modern faces pay great attention to being geometrically precise, and generally have a lot of contrast between thick and thin strokes. Whilst this makes them elegant and attractive in small quantities, it also makes them rather hard to read in lengthy passages, and setting a lot of text in them would wear your readers' eyes out.

So, don't even think of setting a whole book in Bodoni! Even a pamphlet set using this kind of font would be likely to remain unread by most of its recipients. But for headlines or very limited quantities of text (perhaps isolated paragraphs accompanied by lots of illustrations), a contrasty modern face can look very elegant and inviting.

Slab serif: as this class of font was designed for limited use in adverts, it's not surprising that slab serif fonts are rarely considered for use as body text. Some fonts of this type, though, can work well in substantial passages. A geometric slab serif such as Rockwell is of course of little use for reading in large chunks; however, a more humanist style of slab serif such as Clarendon can work very well. You wouldn't set a book in it, but Clarendon is very legible for long passages.

Sans-serif: even though it's tautological, I need to say that sans-serif typefaces have no serifs. By definition, therefore, they are not designed to be used for long passages of text, because serifs exist to guide the eye, and their absence means that sans-serif fonts don't scan as well. (You may not be particularly aware of this on a conscious level, but that doesn't stop it being true!)

On the other hand, the absence of serifs makes the letter shapes very clear, and lends a clean and attractive look to the page. So, a nice, elegant sans-serif face such as Optima looks extremely approachable and fresh, and much more inviting than a heavy, serif-bedecked face which might be more likely to put your readers off. The absence of serifs certainly doesn't make a font illegible; it just makes it less suitable for extended reading. A slight loss of legibility may be balanced by an increased approachability in sans-serif faces. So, if your text is not too extensive, a sans-serif font may be a good choice.

Script, black letter and other styles: it should be pretty obvious when and when not to use these styles of font, so I won't cover them here.

PRACTICAL CONCERNS

So, the kind of work you're doing will influence your choice of font to some extent, and, as a very broad rule of thumb, the more extensive your text, the older should be the style of font family that you use. But part of your choice will also be determined by the output device you expect to use. Are you printing the document out yourself or sending it to a commercial printer? And if you're printing it yourself, how good is your printer? Are you going to use a photocopier to make multiple copies, or print them all yourself? What type of paper are you going to use?

If you're designing your work for professional printing and duplication, then to a large extent you can ignore such practical questions because (unless the job's being done on the cheap) you're going for the best option in terms of quality, and the fine detail in your document isn't going to suffer either at the printing or the reproduction stage. But for smaller jobs that you're going to run off yourself, you do need to have practical matters such as these in mind from the start.

The first concern is your own printer. If you have a laser printer, then you're likely to be fairly safe for most jobs at the initial printing stage (though not at the reproduction stage). Most modern laser printers provide a resolution of at least 600dpi, which is enough to make a good job of reproducing almost all fonts at even small sizes. (Older 300dpi lasers should be used with care for very small text, but are still adequate in most situations.) However, if you're only using an inkjet printer, then crispness is likely to suffer (even with the newest and most expensive models), and you should take care in the fonts you pick. Fonts with very fine hairlines or serifs are not likely to reproduce particularly well, and such fine lines may appear fuzzy or disappear completely. So, part of your font choice will be determined by your printing equipment.

The next stage is reproduction. If you're taking the somewhat less cost-effective option of printing all the copies yourself on your own laser printer, then you're safe; you can use fine lines (and subtle shading in your graphics) to take advantage of your printer. If you're going to photocopy from a laser-printed master, though, the quality issue raises its head again, as a photocopy will never be as good as the original (and it may be awful if the photocopier is poor).

Finally, even with the most expensive printing methods, the quality of paper you use is a factor in itself at all stages. Poor quality or textured paper can cause problems. Unless you are using the best and most appropriate quality of paper for both the printing and reproduction stages, your expectations should not be too high.

So, if your equipment is less than ideal at any stage in the reproduction process, you may need to compensate in your choice of fonts. Pick a font which will not vanish at small sizes; don't use one with thick vertical strokes and fine horizontal ones, as it's likely to end up looking more like a rickety fence than a line of type after it's been through the photocopier. This isn't to say that you should allow the output mechanism to compromise the design process, but it should certainly be something to bear in mind when making your initial choices.

SIZE AND SPACING

Be aware that different font families have different overall widths, and so one family will produce a more condensed appearance than another (even though neither is described as being 'condensed' as such). It's like the fact that two fonts can appear to be of widely differing sizes even though they're both

reproduced at the same point size, as mentioned in the previous section. Just because two fonts are used at 12pt, for example, there's no guaranteeing that they'll both fit the same number of words per line (that's highly unlikely, in fact). Experiment, and see what style suits your project best. If you're producing a magazine, then a slightly condensed face will probably suit you well because it will allow you to get more words on each page. For example, Times New Roman is a more naturally condensed font than Plantin.

Font choice also has an effect on line length. As explained back in section 2, the longer a line of text is, generally the greater should be the space between lines. The choice of font also has some influence on this equation, because the more open and round a typeface is, the more empty space it needs between successive lines. (Wider margins also become important.) A naturally condensed face has a relatively small amount of space within and between the letters, and so the line space used should balance it. As the letters become rounder and more open, the line space needs to grow a little to compensate for this. On the other hand, using a very condensed font on a long line isn't a good idea because it increases the perceived length of the line and makes it harder to read, so getting the balance right between the length of the line and the 'condensedness' of the font is both important and somewhat tricky to do. In the end, though, common sense prevails: use more condensed faces with shorter lines (probably in multiple columns) and more open, rounder fonts with longer lines (maybe on single-column pages).

TARGET YOUR READERSHIP

Is your project serious or fun? Are you trying to draw in lots of people, or are you aiming at a specific, narrow readership whose interest is guaranteed? Your choice of font should be appropriate for the purpose in hand. If your text is highly serious, then a very legible serif face is appropriate, but if you want to draw people in, then pick something more casual. Generally the more distinctive a font is (and the more exotic the twiddly bits it boasts) the more 'casual' it is likely to be, and a casual font can be very inviting and attention-grabbing. As long as you don't go so far as to make your document illegible, a casual font can catch and keep your readers' attention.

Also, decide on how much of your document you expect to be read. If it's a magazine, then you'll hope that it'll be most or all of it, but if it's an advertising pamphlet, it may be only the odd short paragraph or bullet point. If you expect your readers to 'pick and mix' in terms of the bits they read, then you can get away with using more eye-catching and less legible fonts in order to maximise the visual impact of the document.

GET THE MESSAGE ACROSS

And finally, the most important consideration is the one that it's hardest to explain: how to pick a font which best suits the project in hand. Your choice should, if possible, be appropriate to the subject and convey something in its own right. On the other hand, though, you should try to avoid typographical clichés and corny decisions.

For a 'silly' example, if I said "Star Trek" in this context, I bet a lot of readers would think of slanting sans-serif letters with sharp angles and a generally futuristic look. Whilst this style may have become somewhat clichéd in itself because it has been widely copied in recent years, the designer of those on-screen credits back in the 1960s made a good decision: the chosen font was futuristic and suited the subject matter, but it was legible nonetheless, and the designer didn't fall into the trap of being too gimmicky.

On the other hand, consider the much more modern sci-fi TV series, "Babylon 5" (which, aside from its typography, I happen to like enormously). In many instances within this programme, an extremely illegible, angular and broken typeface is seen on-set. This is extremely corny! Here, the designers have fallen into the trap of trying to make something look futuristic through use of unsophisticated and gimmicky imagery. The fact is that legible, old style fonts have already been in use for centuries; they're timeless, and are largely impervious to changing fashions. I hardly think that we'll have abandoned them by the year 2258 (the year in which Babylon 5 is first set).

So, when choosing a font, try to pick one that gets the right feeling across but avoids being too obvious or corny. The best way to learn to do that is to be observant, and to look around at the choices that other designers have already made. Try to decide for yourself why they took their decisions, and whether the results succeed or fail in getting the right message across.

Find out how one of the great secrets of the Universe, the Golden Ratio, relates to DTP

In this final article I am going to talk about the Golden Section. "What's that?" I hear you cry. The answer is that it's one of the most important factors pertaining to good design that has ever been discovered. Artists know all about it, and in fact many designers use it instinctively without ever having heard of it as such, but unless you've had training in formal design it's fairly unlikely that you'll have come across it.

"Golden Section" is in fact a 19th century name for a ratio discovered by Euclid. To explain it properly requires a bit of simple mathematics , but if you find this off-putting, don't worry; all you really need to know in the end is what numbers to punch into your computer to make use of the ratio, so gloss over the next few paragraphs if you wish.

$$\frac{a}{b} = \frac{b}{a + b}$$

This just says that "a is to b as b is to a-plus-b." At its simplest, this can be shown as a straight line: see figure 1.

The remarkable thing about the Golden Section is not just the ratio itself, but the fact that simply by adding on terms it is possible to get an endless series of Golden Ratios in the same way that a Fibonacci sequence is extended; in actual fact, the further one goes along the Fibonacci sequence, the closer the ratios get to the Golden Ratio anyway. What makes the Golden Section so special (its 'divine' characteristic, according to Kepler) is that every ratio is equal to every other.

THE MAGIC NUMBER

Deriving the numerical value of the Golden Ratio involves some scary algebra, and is well outside the scope of this article. Besides, it is by no means necessary to understand the maths: all you really need to know is the magic number, and that's the irrational number *Phi* (Φ). Phi is the only positive number that becomes its own reciprocal by subtracting 1. Because it is an irrational number (like the better-known *pi*, or π), it can only be approximated as a decimal number. It is evaluated by using the formula:

$$\Phi = \frac{1 + \sqrt{5}}{2} = 1{\cdot}618034$$

For practical purposes, we can round this down to 1·618. We also have to remember its reciprocal, 0·618 (the figures after the decimal point are the same in both numbers).

For any given term in the Golden Sequence, multiplying by 1·618 will give the next term in the sequence, and multiplying by 0·618 will give the previous term. This is the key: multiplying any number by 1·618 gives a larger number, and multiplying that larger number by 0·618 gives the smaller number again. So, all this build-up leads to the very simple rule shown in figure 2.

GOLDEN RATIO IN NATURE

All this talk of numbers and sequences may sound dry and uninteresting, but the reason it's so important is that it occurs all over the place in Nature. What's more, it's fundamental to our own innate sense of

Next size up: × by 1·618
Next size down: × by 0·618

Figure 2: Multipliers to find the next 'Golden' size in whatever measurement you're working with

æsthetic balance, which is why I said at the start that many people use it without even knowing about it. Incorporating the Golden Ratio into critical points in a piece of work is very likely to make it just 'feel right'.

As an example of how fundamental the Golden Section is to us all, hold your left hand up in front of your face and look at the side of your first finger. Curl your finger so that you can see more easily where the joints are, and the lengths of the individual bones.

The first section of your finger, from the tip to the joint, is a little shorter than the next section, from the first joint to the knuckle. Compare this part of your finger with the line in figure 1 (which should be of a similar length): the joint is at the Golden Section between fingertip and knuckle!

Now compare the second section of your finger with the third: the knuckle is at the Golden Section of that particular measurement. Next, compare the top of your hand with the base section of your finger. Golden Section again? Compare the length of your entire hand with the length of your forearm. Golden Section? Finish off by comparing the combined length of your hand and forearm with your entire arm. The Golden Section is at the elbow. Convinced?

Fibonacci numbers crop up very widely where the Golden Section is involved. To continue with the finger example, and looking at my own first finger, my nail is 1cm long, as is the section between it and the first joint. So the first section of my finger is 2cm long overall, and it's comprised of two 1cm halves. The second section is 3cm long, and the next, to the base of my finger, is 5cm. The top of my hand doesn't appear to be quite 13cm long, but I'm sure you get the idea...

As natural creatures, we use the Golden Ratio a great deal in our fundamental make-up, and the same is true with other living things. Animals are similarly proportioned, as are plants. Many creatures with spiral shells use the Golden Ratio in the expansion of the spiral. Or think of the intricate patterns formed by the seeds in the head of a sunflower: their distribution is related to the Golden Section and Fibonacci numbers.

GRASPING THE MATHS

To understand what the Golden Section is all about, we have to start with the Fibonacci sequence of numbers. If you can't remember far enough back to your maths lessons at school, the Fibonacci sequence is as follows:

1, 1, 2, 3, 5, 8, 13, 21, 34, 55, ...

In this sequence, each pair of terms is added to produce the next. Other similar variations exist and have their own names (for example, the Lucas sequence begins with the numbers 1, 3, 4, 7, ... and the Evangelist sequence starts off with 2, 5, 7, 12, ...), but they all use the same basic idea of adding each pair of terms to find the next one in the sequence.

Such sequences find their perfect form with the so-called Golden Section, or Golden Ratio. Euclid called it the "extreme and mean ratio" whilst Kepler called it the "sectio divina", but they both referred to the same thing: the unique ratio which makes additive sequences like the Fibonacci one become 'continuous', in that dividing each successive term by its predecessor in the sequence produces exactly the same ratio.

Put another way, the Golden Ratio occurs when a line or shape is divided up in such a way that the small section is to the large as the large section is to the whole. The Golden Ratio can be expressed algebraically as:

Figure 1: The simplest form of the Golden Section

(figure shows line with segments *b*, *a*, and *a + b*)

It's not only in Nature that we encounter the Golden Section: it can be found in all aspects of art and creation (including such apparently disparate subjects as music and architecture), and we ignore it at our peril.

GOLDEN RATIO IN THE ARTS

Composers from Bach to Bartók have made widespread use of the Golden Section in their compositions, and we often find, on analysing a piece of music by an important composer, that the major musical events will often occur at 'Golden' points within a movement or section, and that Fibonacci numbers crop up everywhere.

In visual arts and design, the Golden Section plays just as important a part. Consider painting a picture that looks out to sea and features a yacht as its focal point. Does the yacht go in the exact centre of the picture? No; that would be obvious and crude. It goes a bit to one side, perhaps centred on the Golden Section point along the width of the picture. And what about the line where the sea meets the sky? You'll rarely find this at the exact vertical centre of the picture. Most often it'll be at, or close to, the Golden Section of the picture's height.

Figure 3 gives an example. It's just a holiday snapshot that I took a few years ago (of the bridge at Wasdale Head in the Lake District), but I tried to get the composition right at the time and, as it turned out, my guess was reasonably accurate: the bridge (the focus of the picture) falls at a Golden Section both horizontally and vertically, and is balanced at the diagonally opposite Golden point by a tree. Bear in mind that there will actually be four Golden points within the frame: two along each axis, depending on which edge of the frame you measure from.

Photographers have a famous 'Rule of Thirds' which they use to achieve good composition in pictures: the idea is that you position key objects on intersections of an imaginary 3×3 grid. However, the trick should not really be to think of the 'Rule of Thirds', but rather the 'Rule of Golden Sections'!

All this isn't to say that every piece of art is engineered so that all elements of importance are at Golden points; that's clearly not the case, and trying to apply the Golden Ratio to everything you do would impose far too many restrictions. But it shouldn't be ignored, and creating a design with the Golden Section in mind will often enhance the result and make it 'feel right'.

RELEVANCE TO DTP

So far I haven't said anything specific about DTP, but its relevance should be obvious by now. Quite what use you make of the Golden Section in DTP work is entirely up to you, but

Figure 3: The focal point of this photo is the bridge; note how it is at a Golden Section both horizontally and vertically. Note also that the picture frame is a Golden Rectangle

there are lots of opportunities to use it when laying out and sizing elements of a page.

You could relate graphical elements by making the smallest one 62% the size of the largest one; or apply the ratio to your use of font sizes. Finding the Golden points on a page is particularly useful with posters: put the key element (title or graphic) at a Golden point, then find the Golden point of the larger remaining section, and put a lesser element there; and so on. These are simplistic examples, but they should give you an idea of things to do. For instance, say you want to create a page with a two-column layout, with a 'major' column and a 'minor' column (see back to the discussion of news page layouts in section 1). Making the division between the two columns fall at the Golden Section of their combined width would be a good idea.

PAPER SIZES

At this point you may wonder whether the A-sizes of paper, which increase proportionally while retaining the same ratio, are based on the Golden Section. In fact, they aren't. Each time you move up or down an A-size, the paper area increases or decreases by a factor of 2; the ratio between the short and long edges of the page is 1:√2 (1:1·414214). A Golden Rectangle (use of which would result in a long page) has a ratio of 1:Φ (1:1·618034). The border of figure 3 is a Golden Rectangle (as are the top-right and bottom-left areas): as you can see, although it's a pleasing shape, it isn't the same aspect as A4 paper. Figure 4 illustrates the difference between A-sized paper and sheets based on the Golden Rectangle.

IN CONCLUSION

This article has spent more time talking about what the Golden Section is than suggesting ways of using it, and that was intentional, because the possibilities are endless and apply to all aspects of design. If you were not aware of the Golden Section before, then this article will, I hope, have given you something new to think about. Look out for the 'divine proportion' in all walks of life, and give it at least a little thought when planning your own work. It's often hard to quantify what's wrong with a piece of design that just 'doesn't work', but often the problem will be simply that the designer didn't have a feeling for proportion. By being aware of proportions in general, and the Golden Section in particular, you can bring harmony and balance to your work.

Since this article was first written, a very comprehensive book on the subject of the number Phi has appeared, and it makes enthralling reading: it is *The Golden Ratio* by Mario Livio (Review, ISBN 0-7472-4987-3).

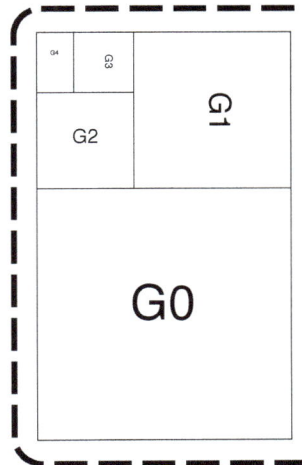
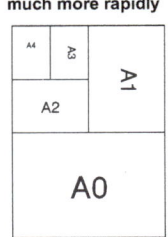

Figure 4: A-sizes of paper increase in size linearly by a factor of 2; Golden Ratio paper (which I have called 'G-size' here) uses a logarithmic scale and so increases in size much more rapidly

G4 G3
G2
G1
G0

A4 A3
A2
A1
A0

www.ingramcontent.com/pod-product-compliance
Lightning Source LLC
Chambersburg PA
CBHW060829290526
45792CB00005BB/1855